WORK IN THE
HEALTH CARE INDUSTRY

by Emma Huddleston

BrightPoint Press

San Diego, CA

BrightPoint Press

© 2020 BrightPoint Press
an imprint of ReferencePoint Press, Inc.
Printed in the United States

For more information, contact:
BrightPoint Press
PO Box 27779
San Diego, CA 92198
www.BrightPointPress.com

LIBRARY OF CONGRESS CATALOGING-IN-PUBLICATION DATA

Names: Huddleston, Emma, author.
Title: Work in the health care industry / by Emma Huddleston.
Description: San Diego, CA : ReferencePoint Press, Inc., [2020] | Series:
    Career finder | Audience: Grades 9 to 12. | Includes index.
Identifiers: LCCN 2019003311 (print) | LCCN 2019005210 (ebook) | ISBN
    9781682827284 (ebook) | ISBN 9781682827277 (hardcover)
Subjects: LCSH: Medicine--Vocational guidance--United States--Juvenile
    literature. | Medical personnel--Vocational guidance--Juvenile literature.
    | Medical care--Vocational guidance--Juvenile literature. | Vocational
    guidance.
Classification: LCC R690 (ebook) | LCC R690 .H8345 2020 (print) | DDC
    610.69023--dc23
LC record available at https://lccn.loc.gov/2019003311

CONTENTS

THE HEALTH CARE INDUSTRY

Doctors and Surgeons

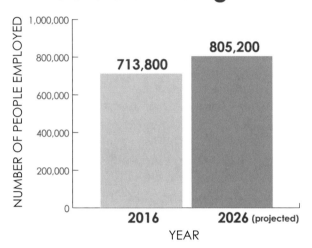

NUMBER OF PEOPLE EMPLOYED

713,800

805,200

2016

2026 (projected)

YEAR

Registered Nurses

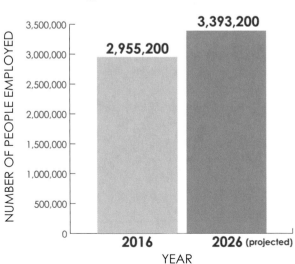

NUMBER OF PEOPLE EMPLOYED

2,955,200

3,393,200

2016

2026 (projected)

YEAR

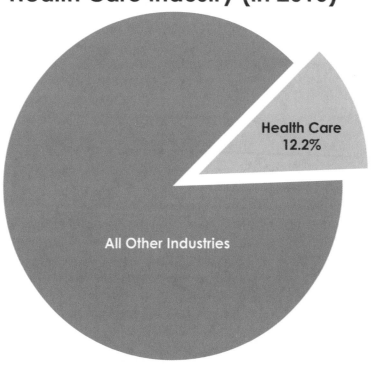

Employment in the
Health Care Industry (in 2016)

Health Care
12.2%

All Other Industries

WHAT IS THE HEALTH CARE INDUSTRY?

Someone coughs near the hospital's entrance. Another person rests a swollen ankle on a chair. The hospital waiting room is full. An assistant at the desk checks people in. A nurse calls out names. She takes people to get their blood drawn. A surgeon nearby prepares for the

At a hospital, many health care professionals work together.

next patient. Everyone works together to

help patients get better.

The health care industry is not limited to

hospitals. Some health care professionals

work in schools and homes. Catching

a cold or getting a checkup are just a

few reasons people may need health care. A variety of health care workers are available to help them.

The four main types of health care jobs are clinical, technical, administrative, and supportive. Clinical and technical jobs include doctors. They can help people with serious needs. Administrative and supportive jobs include assistants and secretaries. They help people with everyday problems.

Supportive health care jobs are the most in-demand jobs in the health care industry. The US population is aging.

Elderly people may need daily help and medical care.

People need more health care as they

get older. However, each type of health

care job is necessary for giving people

well-rounded care.

Health care is a growing job field in the United States. The US Bureau of Labor Statistics predicts that there will be an additional 2.4 million health care jobs by 2026. Health care is also a stable job field. There are many different jobs to choose from. Different jobs have different requirements and salaries. This variety makes health care a great fit for many people.

The health care industry will always be important. Health is a part of life. Health care jobs are rewarding because they help people. Sometimes helping a patient

Health care professionals provide people with quality care and treatment.

is as easy as recommending a new diet.

Sometimes it requires years of aid. Health

care workers are there when people are not

at their best. They change people's lives in

both big and small ways.

CHAPTER ONE

HOME HEALTH AIDE

It can be expensive to visit a doctor, especially if someone needs daily help. That is why home health aides are in demand. Aides care for people in their homes or in a group home. This type of care can be cheaper than visiting a doctor. Aides provide personal care. They help with everyday activities.

MINIMUM EDUCATION: High school diploma or equivalent

PERSONAL QUALITIES: Social, patient, detail-oriented, trustworthy, reliable, caring

CERTIFICATION AND LICENSING: Varies depending on location and employer

WORKING CONDITIONS: Home health aides work in a variety of settings, such as client or group homes.

SALARY: The average salary in 2017 was $23,130 per year, or $11.12 per hour.

NUMBER OF JOBS: 2,927,600 in 2016

FUTURE JOB OUTLOOK: The number of jobs is expected to grow 41% from 2016 to 2026, or an additional 1,208,800 jobs.

A home health aide is the most in-demand job in the health care industry. The need for aides is expected to rise in the next decade. The US population is getting older. About 35 percent of Americans are

Home health aides assist people with daily activities.

fifty years old or older. Many people will

need medical care as they age.

WHAT THEY DO

Aides have many responsibilities. They

assist with daily activities. These activities

can include eating, bathing, dressing, and chores. Sometimes aides buy groceries. They may take clients to doctor appointments. They help organize a client's schedule. Aides make sure clients are taking their medication.

Aides have special relationships with their clients. They may be together for many hours each day. Aides may work in clients' homes. Then clients are in a familiar place. They do not have to travel to get medical care. Aides can get to know the client's family. This can strengthen the relationship between the aide and the client. Aides can

Some home health aides work in group homes and care for many clients.

also work in group homes. Group homes

treat people who need long-term care. This

can include people who have disabilities

or memory loss. In a group home, an aide

might help more than one client each day.

In some states, aides can help with basic medical checks. This includes checking a client's temperature or pulse. Some aides can give clients medication or change their bandages. Aides need to be supervised by a health care professional when doing these tasks. A personal care aide is different from a home health aide. Personal care aides only have training for nonmedical tasks. But they also help clients with daily activities.

Home health aides work with supervisors. Supervisors are other medical professionals, such as nurses. Aides record a client's behavior and progress. They share

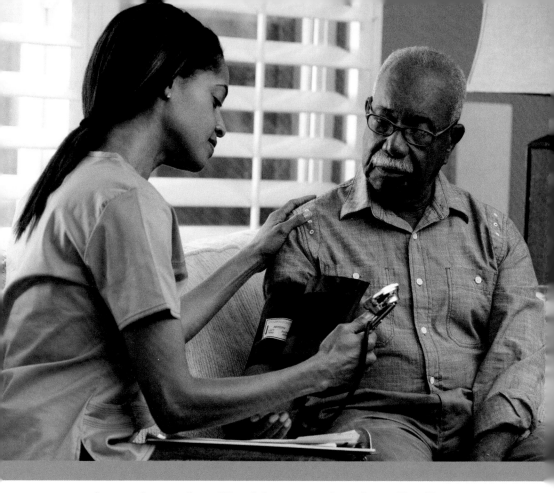

Some home health aides can check a client's blood pressure.

this information with their supervisor. This

information is helpful for doctors. Aides

notice if a client develops new problems.

They help determine if a client needs

different treatment.

Elderly people are common clients. They might have pain that stops them from doing certain activities. They can be forgetful or tired. But aides do not only help elderly people. They also work with people who have lifelong illnesses or disabilities. Some clients may have memory loss.

TRAINING

Aides need a high school degree. A college degree is not required. Some states require aides to go through a training program. But much of the training is done on the job. Aides are trained in many ways. They learn about housekeeping, health, emergencies, and basic safety. Each client has unique needs. Aides need to learn how to meet each client's needs. The client and aide have to adjust to working together. They will be together often.

Most employers require aides to be certified. **Certification** requirements vary from state to state. Aides have to complete at least seventy-five hours of training. Some states require more hours. Community colleges and health care agencies offer training. Aides also have to do sixteen hours of supervised work. They have to pass a written test. Most states also require CPR

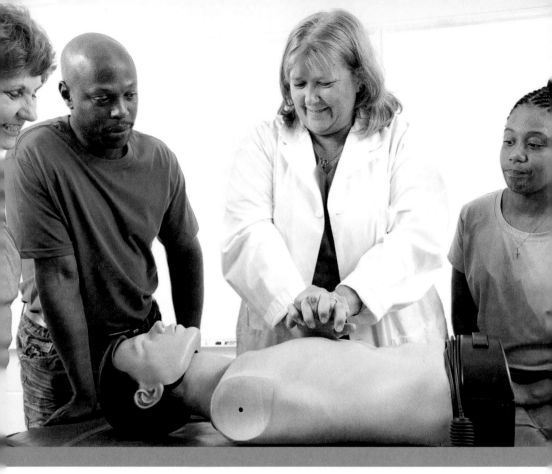

Most home health aides need to have CPR training.

certification. CPR is a way to help people

when their hearts stop beating.

LOOKING AHEAD

Home health aides are in high demand.

Some clients need lifelong care. Others only

need help for a short period of time. Lisa Ecchervaria is a home health aide. She cares for an elderly woman with health problems. She says: "In the time that I have been with [my client], she has become a very special part of my life." Aides often develop close relationships with people. They change people's lives every day. They provide comfort and help to people in need.

FIND OUT MORE

The American Society on Aging (ASA)

website: www.asaging.org

The ASA trains health care professionals who work with elderly clients. It also helps people find jobs in the health care industry. It hosts conferences each year to educate health care professionals.

National Association for Home Care and Hospice (NAHC)

website: www.nahc.org

The NAHC is a network of health care providers, organizations, and businesses. It holds meetings and conferences for health care professionals.

The SCAN Foundation

website: www.thescanfoundation.org

The SCAN Foundation is a charity. It helps elderly people find good health care. It supports people who want to live independently as they age.

CHAPTER TWO

DOCTOR

Doctors are at the core of the health care industry. People go to them for many reasons. People see doctors for regular checkups. Doctors also provide important treatment. They help people who are ill or injured.

WHAT THEY DO

Doctors talk with patients about their health history. Then they examine patients.

MINIMUM EDUCATION: Doctoral or
  professional degree

PERSONAL QUALITIES: Social, organized, caring,
  able to make quick decisions, hardworking, a
  leader, calm under pressure

CERTIFICATION AND LICENSING: State
  license required

WORKING CONDITIONS: Doctors usually work in
  clinics, hospitals, or schools.

SALARY: The average salary in 2017 was $208,000
  per year, or $100 per hour.

NUMBER OF JOBS: 713,800 in 2016

FUTURE JOB OUTLOOK: The number of jobs is
  expected to grow 13% from 2016 to 2026, or an
  additional 91,400 jobs.

An examination can involve taking a

patient's temperature or checking an injury.

Doctors identify any health problems. They

may have the patient go through an X-ray.

X-rays are scans that produce photographs

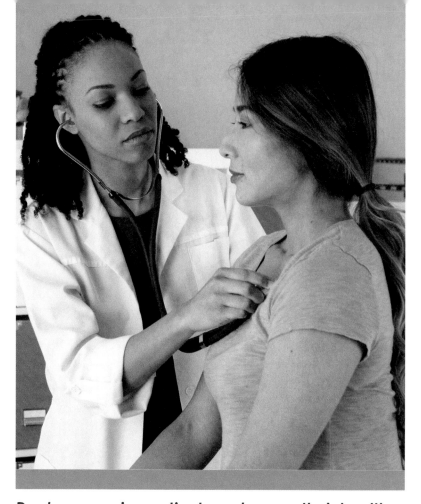

Doctors examine patients and assess their health.

of the inside of a patient's body. This

helps a doctor identify the source of a

health problem.

Doctors find ways to treat patients. They

may **prescribe** medicine. They check in

with patients to make sure the treatment is working. If a treatment is not working, doctors find a new treatment. They try to help patients get better.

Many doctors work in hospitals and **clinics**. They may work odd hours of the day. They sometimes have to be on call. They have to be ready to respond to emergencies outside of their regular working hours. Sometimes they travel to patients' homes.

Doctors work with other health care professionals. These include nurses, physician assistants, and administrative people. These professionals schedule appointments and keep track of patient records. Nurses often help with checkups.

Some doctors work with the same patients for many years. But specialized doctors see new patients all the time. They help people who have a specific illness or injury. During their schooling, most doctors specialize in a certain field. For example, some doctors treat people who are pregnant. They help deliver babies. Other doctors are trained to work with children. They are called pediatricians. Cardiologists are trained to treat heart conditions.

Pediatricians specialize in treating children.

Surgeons are different from doctors
because they operate on patients. They
treat injuries and diseases. Surgery often
happens after problems occur. It can

also be a way to prevent future problems. There are general surgeons and specialty surgeons. Specialty surgeons are trained to treat certain parts of the body, such as the brain or heart.

TRAINING

It takes a lot of training to become a doctor. This job requires the most training of all health care jobs. A bachelor's degree is required. Many students choose science-related fields, such as biology, as their **major**. Then they go through four years of medical school. Getting into medical school can be challenging.

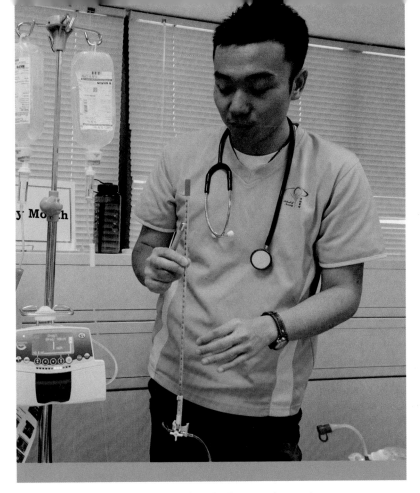

In medical school, students learn how to use special equipment.

A student needs letters of recommendation and volunteer hours. The student needs to pass the Medical College Admission Test (MCAT). This test is difficult. Students need to study a lot to prepare for this test.

The first two years of medical school are mostly spent learning in classrooms. The last two years are mostly spent working in hospitals and clinics. Doctors supervise medical school students. Students work with different types of doctors. This helps students decide which field they might want to specialize in.

The final step in becoming a doctor is residency. Residency is specialized training in a hospital. It can take three to seven years depending on the field.

All doctors and surgeons must be licensed. Licensing requirements

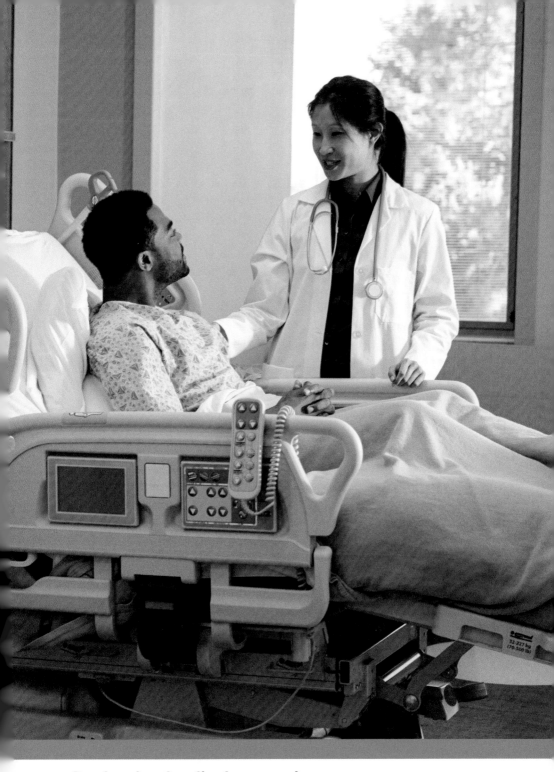

Doctors treat patients every day.

In residency training, people gain experience working in hospitals.

are different in each state. The main requirements are medical school and residency training. People who want to specialize need certification. Certification happens after residency. It includes an additional test. Certification can give a doctor more job opportunities.

LOOKING AHEAD

Becoming a doctor is not easy. Doctors often have to work unusual hours. This schedule can be tiring. Helping people with serious problems can be challenging. Doctors are often under a lot of pressure. But this career is often rewarding.

Kimberly A. Chernoby is a doctor. She says, "There is nothing more gratifying than the genuine thanks of a patient whose life is improved by your care."

The job outlook for doctors is promising. Doctors are always needed. They help future generations. They can find cures or better ways to treat patients. They help people in times of need. They help save lives every day.

FIND OUT MORE

The American Medical Association (AMA)

website: www.ama-assn.org

The AMA is an organization that provides training and licensing for doctors. It also works with government leaders to make laws that protect patients and health care professionals.

The Association of American Medical Colleges (AAMC)

website: www.aamc.org

The AAMC is a nonprofit association. Its members include US medical schools, hospitals, and other health care groups. It educates medical students, cares for patients, and does medical research.

The Federation of State Medical Boards (FSMB)

website: www.fsmb.org

The FSMB provides tools and resources for health care professionals. It also helps create licensing standards.

CHAPTER THREE

PHYSICIAN ASSISTANT

Physician assistants (PAs) help doctors and surgeons treat patients. They have important jobs. Doctors and surgeons need smart, skilled PAs.

WHAT THEY DO

PAs work in all areas of medicine. They work on a team. The team includes doctors and surgeons. It also includes other health

MINIMUM EDUCATION: Master's degree

PERSONAL QUALITIES: Social, caring, hardworking, detail-oriented, calm under pressure

CERTIFICATION AND LICENSING: State license required

WORKING CONDITIONS: Physician assistants work in doctor's offices, hospitals, care centers, or schools.

SALARY: The average salary in 2017 was $104,860 per year, or $50.41 per hour.

NUMBER OF JOBS: 106,200 in 2016

FUTURE JOB OUTLOOK: The number of jobs is expected to grow 37% from 2016 to 2026, or an additional 39,600 jobs.

care professionals. PAs can do many of

the same tasks a doctor or surgeon can

do. They can examine patients. They can

prescribe medicine. They may also help

stitch up patients after surgery. But PAs

Physician assistants help treat patients.

need supervision. Doctors and surgeons

supervise PAs.

PAs are similar to nurses. But PAs may

have a different focus. Nurses are trained

to focus on the patient. PAs are trained to focus more on the medical issues.

Most PAs work in doctor's offices. Others work in hospitals and schools. PAs often work unusual hours. They may work on nights, weekends, or holidays. Like doctors, PAs can be put on call. They have to be ready to help in emergencies.

TRAINING

Many people who become PAs first work as nurses or paramedics. Paramedics help people in emergencies. These jobs give people experience in patient care. Becoming a nurse requires a degree and training. Nurses also need a special license. Becoming a paramedic requires training. Paramedics need a special license too.

There are other ways to get experience. People can volunteer at hospitals or clinics. This can help them get accepted into PA education programs.

Most PA programs take two years to complete. Students earn a master's degree. They take classes. They do clinical rotations. A clinical rotation is training with a doctor. Students train with different types of doctors. This helps them learn what they

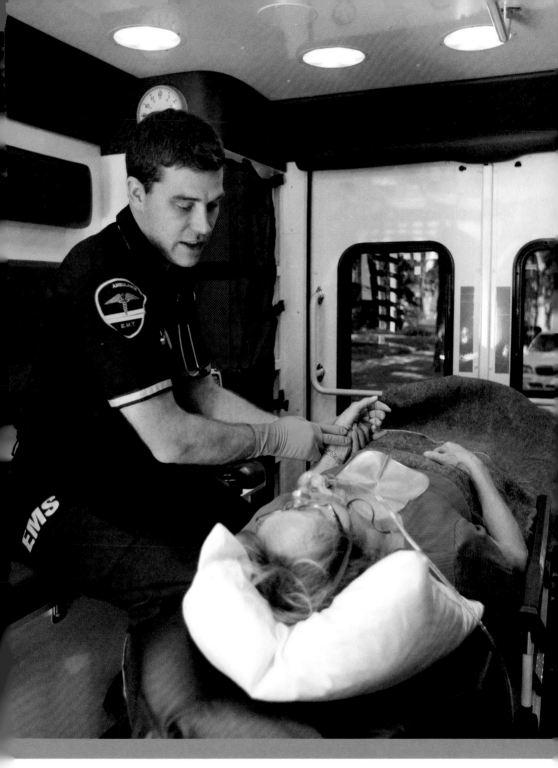

Paramedics treat people in emergencies.

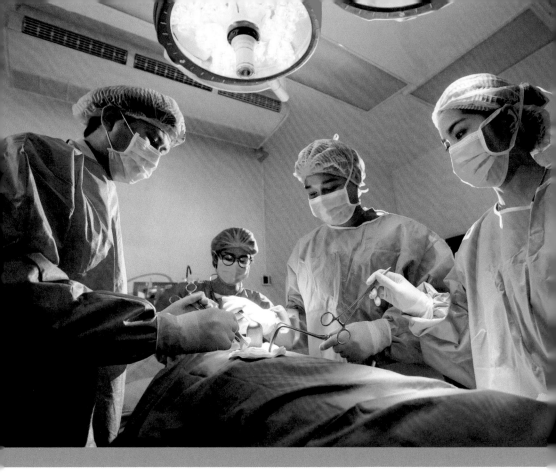

Some PAs are trained to help surgeons perform surgeries.

are most interested in. Some rotations lead

to a job. Doctors may hire students as PAs

after working with them in a rotation.

All PAs in the United States must be

licensed. They must graduate from a PA

program. Then they need to pass the

Physician Assistant National Certifying

Exam. They need to take one hundred

hours of classes every two years to stay

certified. They also need to take an exam

every ten years.

PAs can work in any health care field.

Some PAs work with pediatricians. Others

help doctors deliver babies. PAs can

change their specialization throughout

their career. It is easier for PAs to change

this than it is for doctors. PAs need less

training than doctors. The job is a great fit

for people who want to explore different

areas of health care. Dawn Morton-Rias is president of the National Commission on Certification of Physician Assistants. She says, "Certified PAs enjoy flexibility, a work/life balance, and an above-average starting salary."

LOOKING AHEAD

PAs are in high demand. The work of a PA is rewarding. PAs may work with patients for many years. They develop strong relationships with patients. They provide important medical care.

FIND OUT MORE

The American Academy of Physician Assistants (AAPA)

website: www.aapa.org

The AAPA is a national organization. It helps students become PAs by connecting them to job opportunities. It also works with government leaders on health care issues.

The National Commission on Certification of Physician Assistants (NCCPA)

website: www.nccpa.net

The NCCPA sets standards for PA programs in the United States. It provides important resources for PAs, such as practice exams.

The Physician Assistant Education Association (PAEA)

website: www.paeaonline.org

The PAEA provides information about PA programs. It supports and furthers education for PAs.

CHAPTER FOUR

REGISTERED NURSE

Registered nurses (RNs) are an important part of the health care industry. They work with doctors. They make sure patients get the treatment they need. RNs also help patients feel comfortable. They talk to patients. They use special equipment. The equipment helps them monitor patients.

MINIMUM EDUCATION: Associate's degree

PERSONAL QUALITIES: Social, caring, hardworking, detail-oriented, calm under pressure

CERTIFICATION AND LICENSING: License required

WORKING CONDITIONS: Nurses work in hospitals, doctor's offices, care centers, or schools.

SALARY: The average salary in 2017 was $70,000 per year, or $33.65 per hour.

NUMBER OF JOBS: 2,955,200 in 2016

FUTURE JOB OUTLOOK: The number of jobs is expected to grow 15% from 2016 to 2026, or an additional 438,100 jobs.

WHAT THEY DO

RNs have many tasks. They observe and record a patient's **symptoms**. They give some treatments such as shots. They also operate medical equipment. They use machines that monitor a patient's vital signs.

Vital signs are signs that organs are working properly. Heartbeat and breathing are examples of vital signs.

RNs check on patients when doctors are busy. They talk with patients' families. They explain a patient's treatment. Some patients need additional care after going home. RNs show family members how to give treatments at home.

Most RNs work on a team with doctors. Some work with a specific group of patients. Neonatal nurses care for newborn babies. Public health nurses educate people about health care. Pediatric

Neonatal nurses are trained to treat newborn babies. Newborns need special treatment and care.

oncology nurses work with children who have cancer.

RNs work with a variety of patients. They work in different locations. Hospitals and clinics need nurses at all times. Some

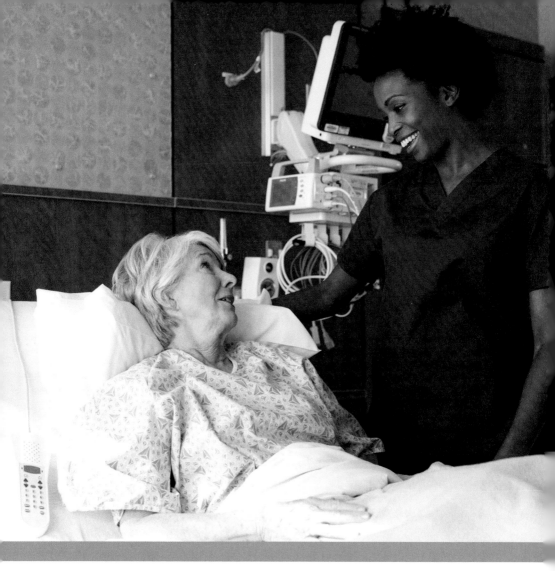

RNs help treat patients and make them feel comfortable.

RNs work odd hours or on holidays.

Sometimes they need to be on call to help

with emergencies.

TRAINING

There are different types of nurses.

Licensed practical nurses (LPNs) do basic

medical care. They check patients' blood

pressure. They record health issues. They

may change a patient's bandage. Other

nurses and doctors supervise LPNs. People

need education and a license to become

an LPN. The education program must

be approved by the state. LPN programs

usually take one year to complete. People

must pass an exam to earn an LPN license.

RNs supervise LPNs. They also assist

doctors and surgeons. They help perform

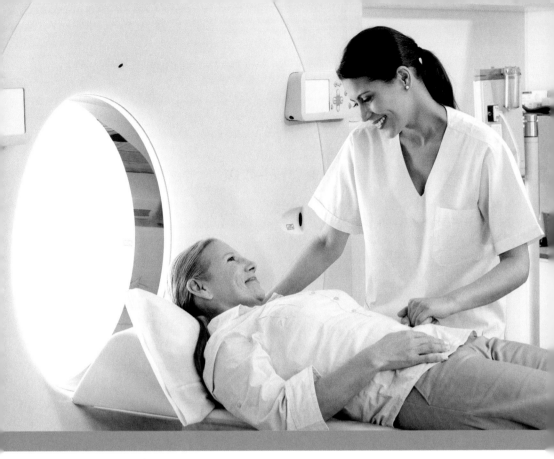

Some nurses specialize in radiology. They treat patients who undergo diagnostic imaging procedures, such as CT scans.

tests. They talk with doctors about test

results and treatments. An RN needs an

associate's degree in nursing (ADN). An

ADN usually takes two years to complete.

Many RNs have a bachelor's degree in

nursing (BSN). A BSN takes four years to complete. Colleges offer ADN and BSN programs.

All nursing programs give students experience. They spend time in hospitals or clinics. Additionally, RNs must be licensed. They must pass a special exam to get this license. It is called the National Council Licensure Examination.

Nurse practitioners (NPs) are specialized RNs. They work directly under a doctor or surgeon. They help **diagnose** and treat patients. NPs have a master's degree in nursing (MSN). An MSN takes two years

Nurses can give people shots.

to complete. Many people complete their MSN while working as an RN. They have to pass an exam to become an NP. Most states require NPs to get a second license related to their field.

LOOKING AHEAD

RNs are always needed. They have important jobs. They provide comfort and care. They help patients with medical tasks. People who want to become a nurse have many different options. There are more than one hundred different nursing specialties.

Nurses work hard. They face many challenges. They also often work long hours. But the job can be rewarding. Nancy Whitt has been a nurse for more than forty-five years. She says, "I have a great job. . . . I make a good salary, and I get to make people's lives a little better."

FIND OUT MORE

The American Nurses Association (ANA)

website: www.nursingworld.org

The ANA provides nurses with certification and training.

The American Society of Registered Nurses (ASRN)

website: www.asrn.org

The ASRN connects nurses to other health care professionals. It offers educational events. It gives guidance to RNs who want to become specialized.

The National Council of State Boards of Nursing (NCSBN)

website: www.ncsbn.org

The NCSBN provides education and resources to people who want to become nurses. It also promotes safe nursing practices in the United States.

CHAPTER FIVE

DIETITIAN

Dietitians are experts on **nutrition**. They often use their skills outside of clinics. Some dietitians work with food companies. They understand how food affects the human body.

WHAT THEY DO

Dietitians help people make smart diet choices. People with food allergies or illnesses might need to change their diet.

MINIMUM EDUCATION: Bachelor's degree

PERSONAL QUALITIES: Caring, communicative, organized, a problem solver

CERTIFICATION AND LICENSING: License required in many states

WORKING CONDITIONS: Dietitians work in hospitals, clinics, or offices.

SALARY: The average salary in 2017 was $59,410 per year, or $28.56 per hour.

NUMBER OF JOBS: 68,000 in 2016

FUTURE JOB OUTLOOK: The number of jobs is expected to grow 15% from 2016 to 2026, or an additional 9,900 jobs.

For example, diabetes is a common disease. It affects how a person's body digests sugar. More than 30 million people in the United States have diabetes. People with diabetes need to stick to special diets. They need to watch their sugar intake.

Dietitians help people find and stick to healthy diets.

Dietitians can help them find the right diet.

Dietitians can also help people who are at

risk for diabetes. Diabetes can be **genetic**.

People with diabetes in the family may have

a higher risk. Dietitians can help them stick to a healthy diet. A healthy diet may help prevent diabetes.

Some dietitians work in hospitals. Others work for health companies or organizations. They meet with clients. They review a client's health history. They see if a client's family has a history of health issues. Some health issues can be prevented. A healthy diet and exercise may help.

Dietitians talk with clients about eating habits. They give clients advice about their diets. They help the client set goals. Then they help the client reach these goals.

Dietitians educate people about different types of foods and diets.

They make meal plans. Sometimes they recommend exercises. Exercises can help the client stay healthy.

There are different types of dietitians. Clinical dietitians work in hospitals or clinics. They treat people's health issues with dietary changes. They can become specialized. For example, some work with people who have digestive problems. Others work with people who have diabetes. Still others may work with clients who have kidney disease.

Community dietitians work with the public. They give speeches or host events.

They educate people about healthy diets. They talk about other ways to stay healthy too. Some dietitians work in grocery stores or supermarkets. They talk to shoppers. They give nutritional advice.

Management dietitians are another type of dietitian. They work in cafeterias, hospitals, prisons, and schools. They plan food programs for large groups. Sometimes they are in charge of kitchen staff.

TRAINING

Many states require dietitians to be certified as registered dietitian nutritionists (RDNs). An RDN must first have a bachelor's

Some dietitians help create healthy meal plans for students.

degree. Many students major in dietetics. They may also study clinical nutrition or public health. They have to complete a dietetic **internship**. In an internship, a dietitian supervises and trains a student. Students need more than 1,200 hours of supervised training.

Many dietetic internships are available. Some are **accredited**. Others are not. The Accreditation Council for Education in Nutrition and Dietetics regulates US dietitian programs. An accredited internship is required for an RDN certification.

Dietitians can influence the foods people buy.

Fresh foods are important for healthy diets.

People also have to take an exam.

The Commission on Dietetic Registration

gives this exam. People need to pass

this exam to earn their RDN certification.

Dietitians need new training every five years

to remain an RDN.

LOOKING AHEAD

Dietitians have important jobs. They work

in both hospital and community settings.

They help people make smart choices.

They help change people's lives. Their work

can have a widespread impact. Dietitians

who educate the public may affect the food

people buy. This can influence the food

industry. Food companies may respond by making more healthful food options.

People of all ages and lifestyles need dietitians. Knowledge about health and nutrition is important. Barbara Ruhs is a dietitian. She thinks it is important for dietitians to share their knowledge. She says, "The potential to improve public health is huge."

FIND OUT MORE

The Academy of Nutrition and Dietetics
website: www.eatright.org

The Academy of Nutrition and Dietetics is the world's largest organization of nutrition professionals. It works with governments on health issues. It provides health care professionals with information.

The National Association of Nutrition Professionals (NANP)
website: www.nanp.org

The NANP offers resources and information for nutritionists.

INTERVIEW WITH A PROFESSIONAL

Dr. Elsa Kracke is a pediatrician. She works for St. Luke's Children's Pediatrics in Boise, Idaho.

WHY DID YOU BECOME A PHYSICIAN/PEDIATRICIAN?

I always liked science and math growing up, but during high school when I was a student athlete I became interested in nutrition, anatomy, and how the body works. I chose to become a doctor to help others learn how to take care of their bodies, so they can prevent illnesses. Being a doctor is fun because you get to help children every day.

CAN YOU DESCRIBE YOUR TYPICAL WORK DAY?

A typical work day includes going to the clinic and seeing patients from infancy to eighteen years old. I see children for well child checks to monitor their growth and developmental milestones (such as walking and talking) and check their vision and hearing. I also help children when they are sick or injured. I work with a team of people, including nurses, therapists, and social workers.

WHAT DO YOU LIKE MOST ABOUT YOUR JOB?

I like seeing kids every day and hearing about what new things they are learning in school, finding out about the new activities they are participating in after school, and showing them how much they have grown. When kids are sick, I like treating them and helping them get better. I also like to educate families on the importance of vaccinations to prevent them from getting sick.

WHAT PERSONAL QUALITIES DO YOU FIND MOST VALUABLE FOR THIS TYPE OF WORK?

Qualities important to becoming a doctor include a hard work ethic, attention to detail, and some perseverance. When you are a doctor, you will continue to need those qualities in addition to being empathic [understanding and caring] and always keeping an open mind.

WHAT ADVICE DO YOU HAVE FOR STUDENTS WHO MIGHT BE INTERESTED IN THIS CAREER?

Becoming a doctor is a long process, but if you set short-term goals and keep working hard the time will go by quickly. Also, read as much as you can as often as you can. Reading teaches you so much not only about medicine but also about different walks of life and how to relate to all patients.

OTHER JOBS IN THE HEALTH CARE INDUSTRY

- Audiologist
- Dentist
- Diagnostic Imaging Worker
- Emergency Medical Technician (EMT)
- Exercise Physiologist
- Massage Therapist
- Medical Assistant
- Medical Laboratory Scientist
- Medical Transcriptionist
- Nursing Assistant
- Nutritionist
- Occupational Therapist
- Occupational Therapy Assistant or Aide
- Optician
- Optometrist
- Paramedic
- Personal Care Aide
- Pharmacist
- Phlebotomist
- Physical Therapist
- Podiatrist
- Prosthetist
- Radiologic and MRI Technician
- Recreational Therapist
- Speech-Language Pathologist
- Surgeon

Editor's Note: The US Department of Labor's Bureau of Labor Statistics provides information about hundreds of career options. The agency's Occupational Outlook Handbook describes the education and skill requirements, pay, and future outlook for each job. The Occupational Outlook Handbook can be found online at www.bls.gov/ooh.

GLOSSARY

accredited
recognized as meeting certain requirements or standards

certification
an official recognition from a state or an organization that shows someone has special training

clinic
a place where people can get medical treatment, usually for minor injuries or illnesses

diagnose
to identify a disease or illness based on a patient's symptoms

genetic
able to be passed from a parent to a child

internship
a period of training or work to learn about a certain job

major
the main subject a student studies at a college or university

nutrition
the food and nutrients people need to grow and stay healthy

prescribe
to give a prescription, or a note that gives information about the drugs and medicine a person needs

symptom
a sign that someone may have a disease or illness

INDEX

ABOUT THE AUTHOR

Emma Huddleston lives in the Twin Cities with her husband. She enjoys writing children's books, but she likes reading novels even more. When she is not writing or reading, she likes to stay active by running and swing dancing. She thinks careers in health care are some of the most important jobs in the world.